We are **pediatric neuropsychologists.**
What a mouthful, right? It basically means we are "thinking doctors" for kids.

We work with children of all ages to understand how they think and learn. To do that, we spend lots of time talking with them and the important people in their lives, like their parents and teachers.

We also have them do different activities, like solving puzzles and math problems, building with blocks, looking at pictures, answering questions, reading and writing, and playing word and memory games.

Different Thinkers
ADHD

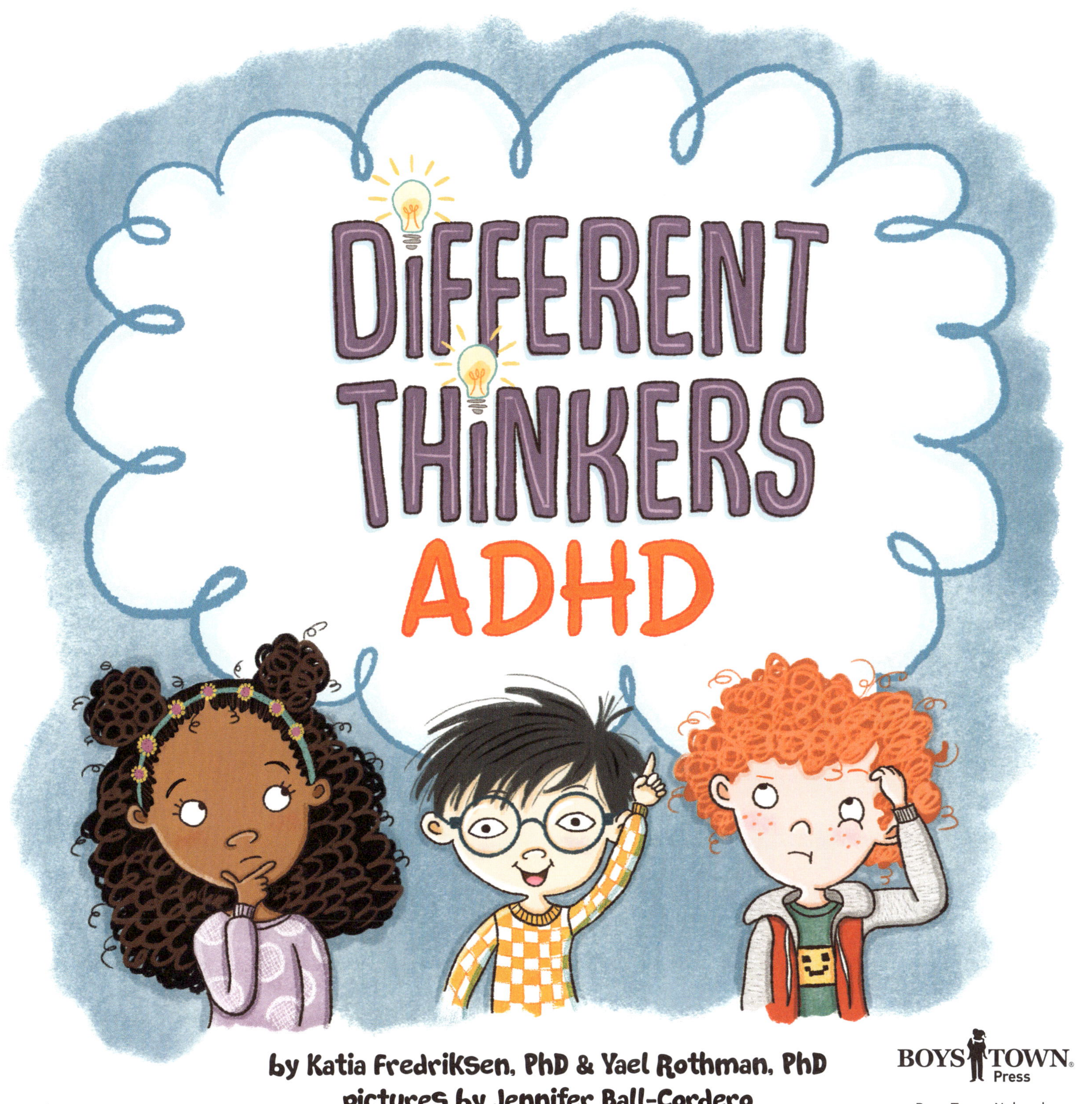

by Katia Fredriksen, PhD & Yael Rothman, PhD
pictures by Jennifer Ball-Cordero

BOYS TOWN Press
Boys Town, Nebraska

DIFFERENT THINKERS: ADHD

ISBN: 979-8-88907-006-1 (PB), ISBN: 979-8-88907-010-8 (HC)

Published by Boys Town Press, 13603 Flanagan Blvd.,
Boys Town, NE 68010

For a Boys Town Press catalog, call **1-800-282-6657**
or visit our website: **BoysTownPress.org**

Publisher's Cataloging-in-Publication Data

Names: Fredriksen, Katia, author. | Rothman, Yael, author. | Ball-Cordero, Jennifer, illustrator.

Title: Different thinkers: ADHD / by Katia Fredriksen, PhD & Yael Rothman, PhD ; pictures by Jennifer Ball-Cordero.

Other title: ADHD.

Identifiers: 979-8-88907-006-1 (paperback) | ISBN: 979-8-88907-010-8 (hardcover)

Subjects: LCSH: Attention-deficit hyperactivity disorder--Juvenile literature. | Attention-deficit hyperactivity disorder--Treatment--Juvenile literature. | Attention-deficit-disordered children--Juvenile literature. | Hyperactive children--Juvenile literature. | Parents of attention-deficit-disordered children--Handbooks, manuals, etc. | Neurodiversity--Juvenile literature. | Self-esteem--Juvenile literature. | Child mental health--Juvenile literature. | CYAC: Attention-deficit hyperactivity disorder. | Hyperactive children. | Neurodiversity. | Self-esteem. | Emotions. | Mental health. | BISAC: JUVENILE NONFICTION / Disabilities. | JUVENILE NONFICTION / Neurodiversity. | JUVENILE NONFICTION / SOCIAL TOPICS / Self-Esteem & Self-Reliance. | JUVENILE NONFICTION / HEALTH & DAILY LIVING / Mental Health. | JUVENILE FICTION / Disabilities.

Classification: LCC: RJ506.H9 F74 2024 | DDC: 618.92/8589--dc23

Printed in the United States
10 9 8 7 6 5 4 3

Boys Town Press is the publishing division of Boys Town, a national organization serving children and families.

More Praise for *Different Thinkers: ADHD*

"Finally! A book that explains ADHD to the elementary school set in a super-relatable and super-readable format. Different Thinkers: ADHD *is filled with real-life examples that draw the reader in as well as strategies and conversation starters for parents and educators to use. The authors, Drs. Fredriksen and Rothman, pepper the book with reminders that children with ADHD are not flawed nor alone, have both strengths and challenges, and, most importantly, that different thinkers help move the world forward!"*

– LESLIE JOSEL, *ADDitude* magazine's "Dear ADHD Family Coach" columnist

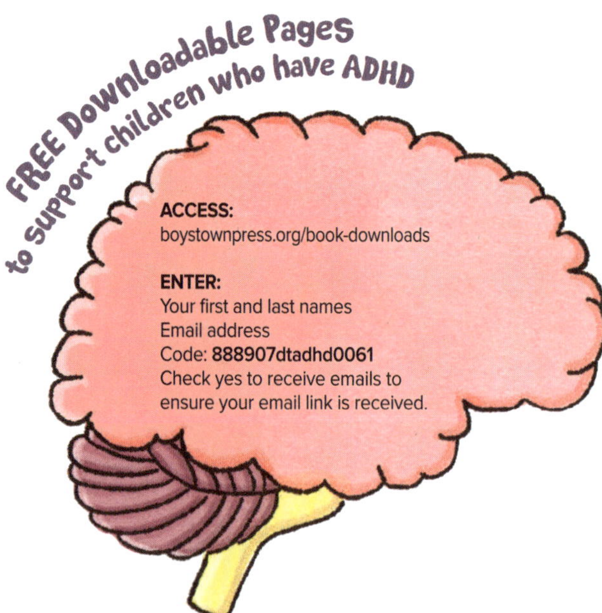

Games and activities help us discover how kids think, learn, and feel. We then use that information to make a plan that will help children solve or manage whatever challenges or problems they face.

A very important part of this process is helping kids learn more about how their amazing brains work, so they (and their families) can understand what is easier and harder for them and why.

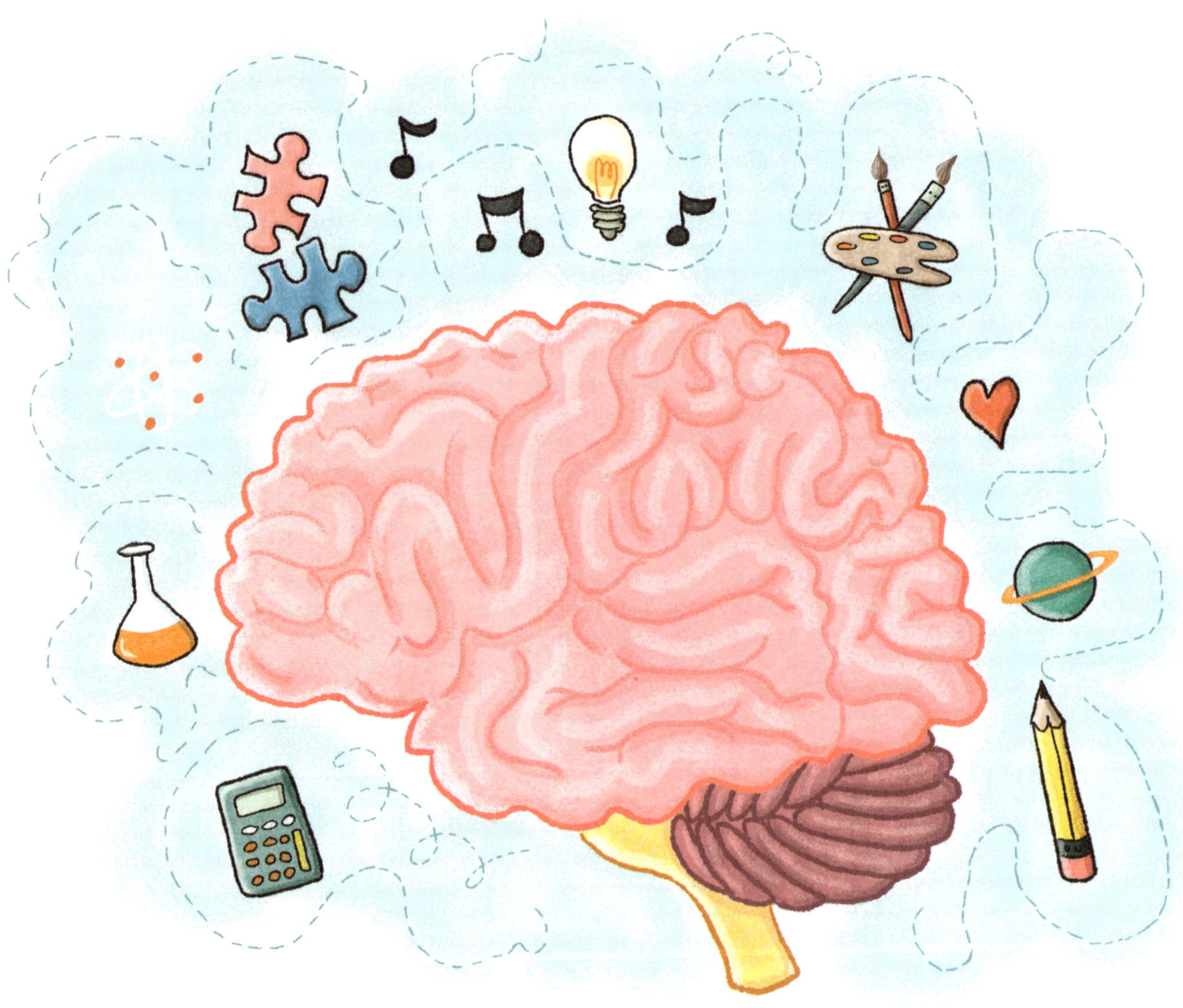

In case you were curious... yes, we are parents too.

Watching our own kids grow, learn, struggle, and thrive really helps us understand all the highs and lows you and your family go through.

Have you ever wondered what's inside your head? If you could peek inside, you would find the most important organ in your body – your amazing brain!

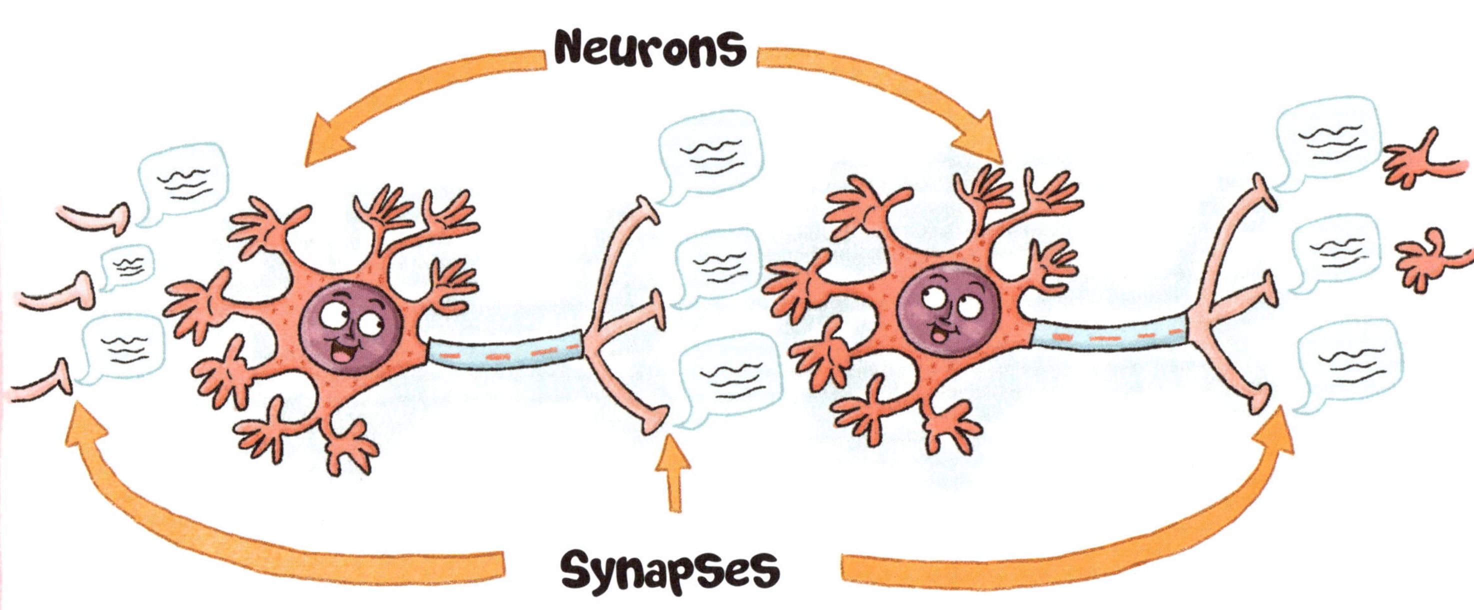

It is made up of billions of tiny brain cells called **neurons** [pronounced nUr-ons] that communicate with each other through connections called **synapses** [pronounced sin-apps-Es].

There are three main parts of the brain:

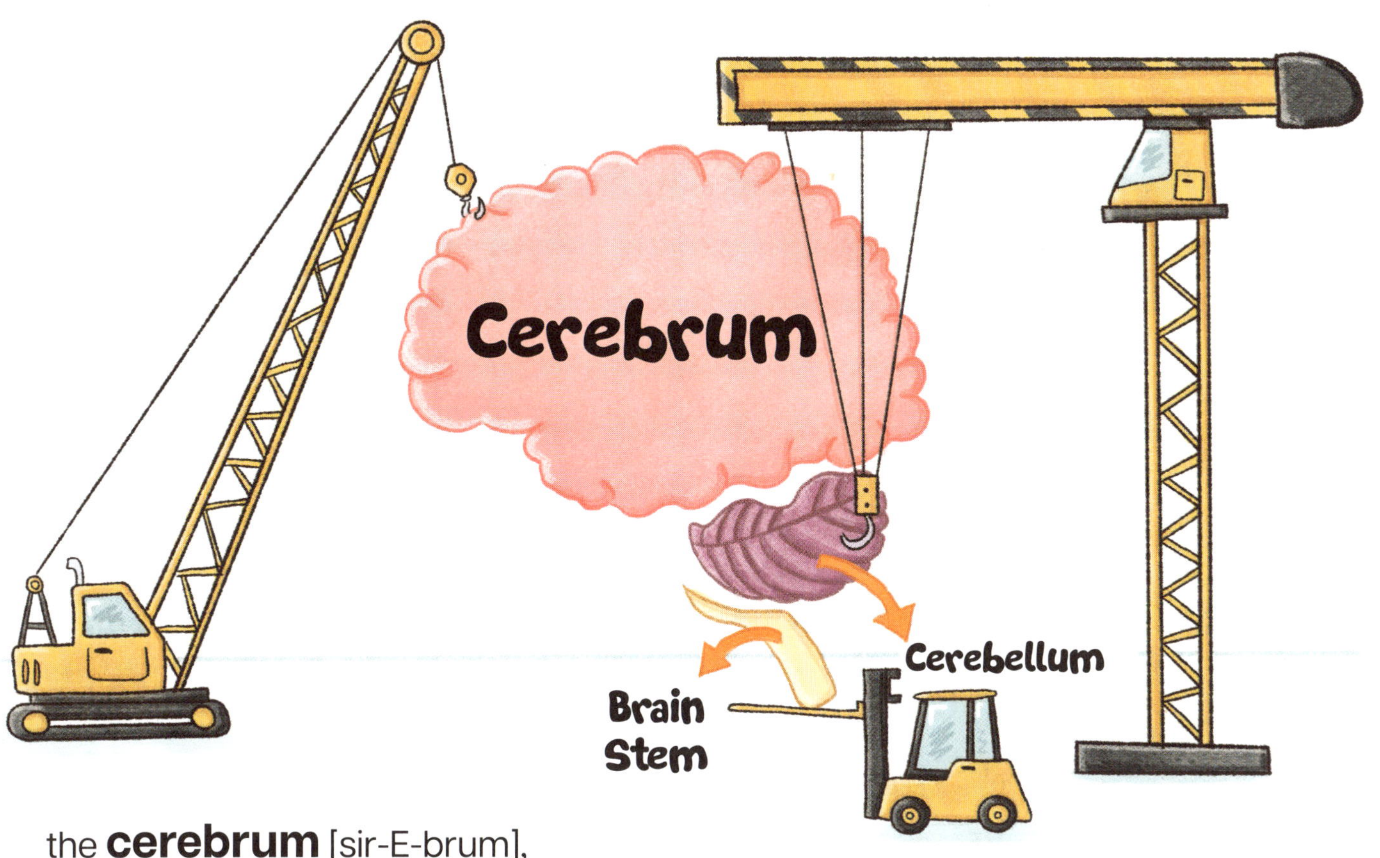

the **cerebrum** [sir-E-brum],
the **cerebellum** [ser-uh-bell-um],
and the **brain stem**.

The cerebrum is the biggest part of your brain. It has two halves, called hemispheres. Each hemisphere is divided into four smaller parts called lobes.

Each lobe has important jobs to do.

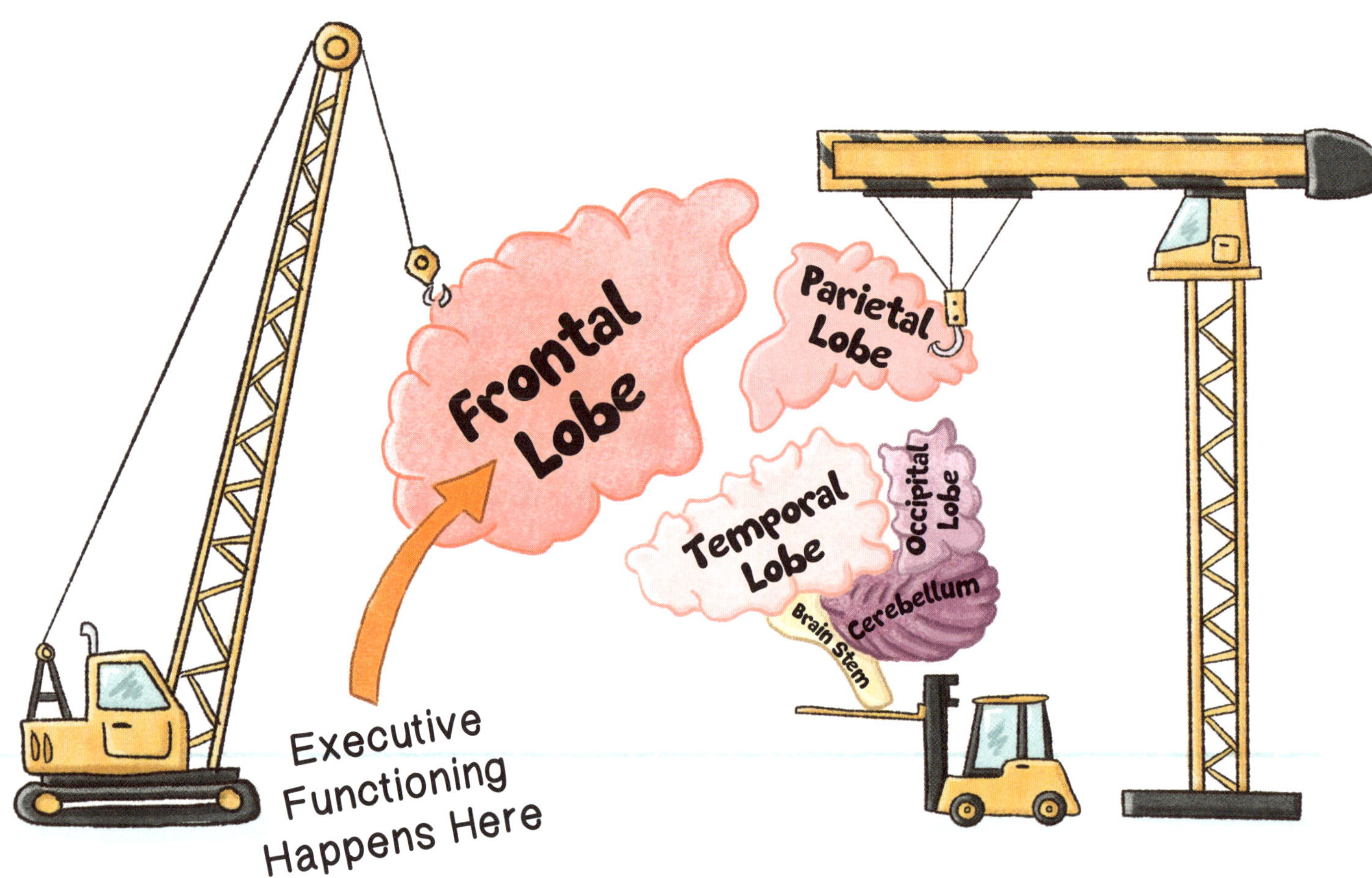

For example, the **frontal lobe** helps you plan ahead, pay attention, and solve problems. It also plays an important role in how you move and talk.

There's also a lot going on in the middle of your brain.

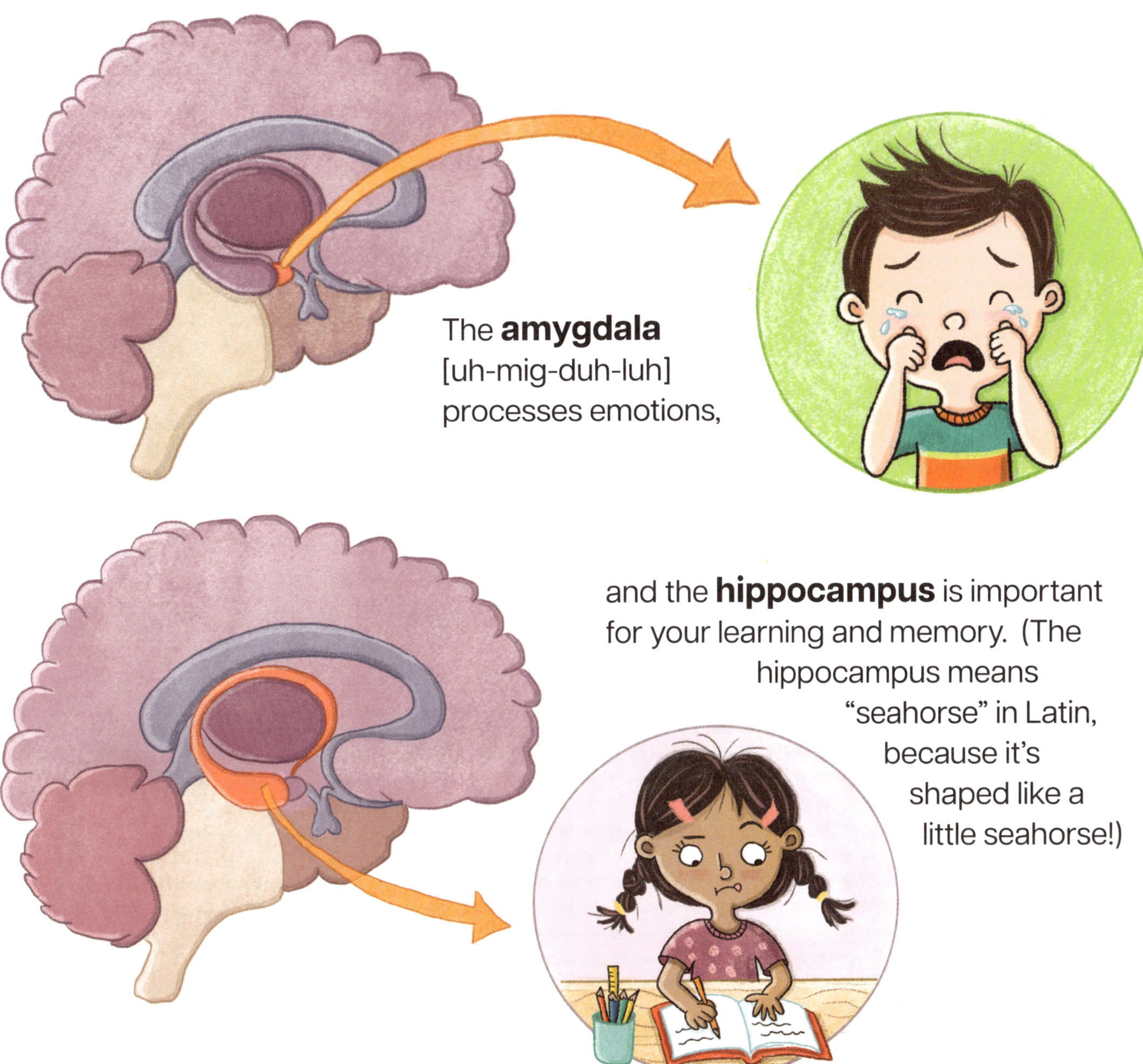

The **amygdala** [uh-mig-duh-luh] processes emotions,

and the **hippocampus** is important for your learning and memory. (The hippocampus means "seahorse" in Latin, because it's shaped like a little seahorse!)

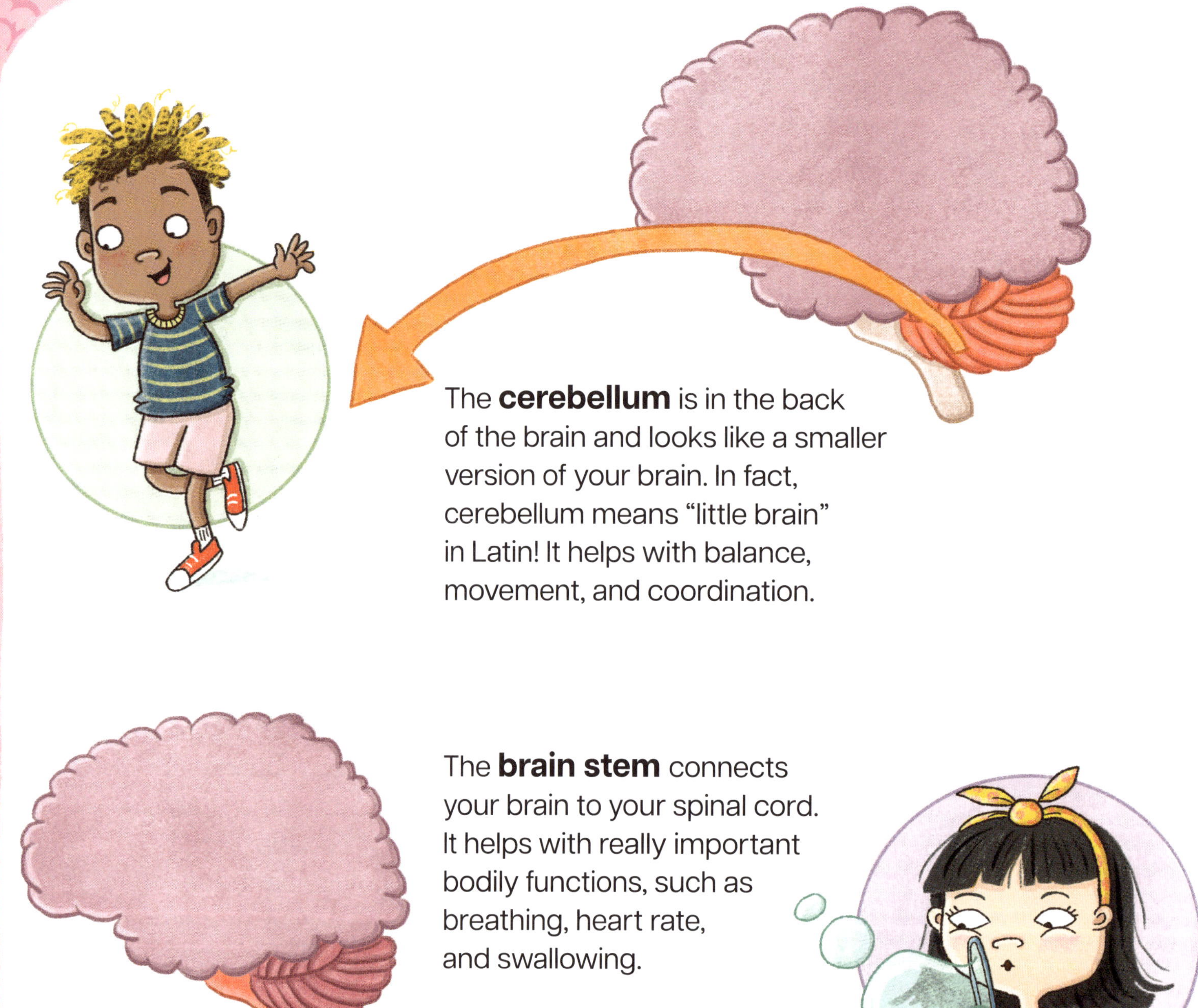

The **cerebellum** is in the back of the brain and looks like a smaller version of your brain. In fact, cerebellum means “little brain” in Latin! It helps with balance, movement, and coordination.

The **brain stem** connects your brain to your spinal cord. It helps with really important bodily functions, such as breathing, heart rate, and swallowing.

Did you know your brain is still a work in progress?

It will keep developing and growing until you reach your early thirties. As you learn new things, your brain makes new connections and strengthens the connections that already exist. Isn't that amazing!

Now that you know the parts of your brain, we want to introduce you to three new friends and explore how they think and learn.

Hey, great to meet you. I'm James.

I like riding my scooter, playing with LEGO blocks, and baking awesome chocolate chip cookies.

Hi, I'm Sammy.

I love to draw my own comics, play video games, and swim at the pool with my brother.

Hola! I’m Ella.

I love to play the flute, do gymnastics, and play with my hamster.

It seems like James, Sammy, and Ella don’t have anything in common – but they do! They are all different thinkers – like you! Each has their own unique way of navigating through the world.

It’s hard for me to get ready for school in the morning because I always start playing with my toys. I forget sometimes to get dressed and go downstairs for breakfast. My big sister gets mad waiting for me. Mom gets grumpy too.

Does this ever happen to you?

I love running, laughing, and shouting with my friends during recess. Other kids like to play quiet games, like pretend family. My favorite game is tag, and I'm a super-fast chaser. I get really excited when I catch other players, but sometimes they get mad at me. And sometimes I get mad at them too.

Does this ever happen to you?

There is so much to learn at school! Everyone says I'm smart. I try to get good grades and make my parents and teachers proud. But sometimes during class I think about my favorite book. I imagine I'm the main character, waving my wand, casting spells, and going on adventures.

Does this ever happen to you?

We are all different, but we do have something in common.

Self-regulation

is hard for us.

Struggling with self-regulation means we might have trouble paying attention to things, like schoolwork, that other people want us to focus on. Sometimes we might have trouble controlling our behavior, like sitting still, keeping our hands to ourselves, and being quiet when we are supposed to. Other times, it's hard for us to keep our emotions under control when we get upset.

Another thing we may have trouble with is **executive functioning**. That means we might forget to hand in our homework, give our parents a permission slip, or study for a test. We may have trouble getting started on and finishing our homework without help from a grown-up. We may always be running late for things, like soccer practice or birthday parties, and we may have trouble remembering where we left our stuff.

Remember the brain picture on page 6? Executive function skills are located in the frontal lobe. This part of your brain doesn't finish developing until you're an adult, so you still have plenty of growing left to do!

When self-regulation and executive function problems get in the way of our ability to be successful at home, at school, or in other places, like the playground, it might mean we have ADHD.

ADHD stands for **Attention Deficit Hyperactivity Disorder.**

ADHD means having trouble with one or more of the following:

1. Paying attention to things that aren't interesting to us (sometimes called ADD or Attention Deficit Disorder)
2. Sitting still, without fidgeting, squirming, or standing up
3. Thinking before we act

Kids like us, who have ADHD, are different thinkers,

which means we may have special ways of seeing and doing things. The world was not built for different thinkers, so there are some things that can be harder for kids like us.

But being a different thinker can also be an amazing thing. Different thinkers help move the world forward. We see things differently, so we can come up with new ideas, inventions, art, and more.

Kids with ADHD have lots of strengths.

We can really focus on and stick with activities that are important to us, which can help us gain a lot of knowledge or develop more advanced skills. For example, James builds the most amazing creations.

We often have an adventurous spirit and are excited to try new things and create. We are spontaneous, energetic, and fun-loving. For example, Ella has a fantastic imagination and loves telling stories. And Sammy is passionate about his art.

ADHD can sometimes look a little different in boys and girls.

Boys may have more trouble controlling their behavior, which makes their ADHD more visible. Girls may find it harder to pay attention, which isn't always as noticeable.

Do you know anyone with ADHD?

You probably do and don't even realize it. Millions of kids and adults have ADHD! You might have a family member with ADHD because it often runs in families. Or maybe you know about a famous person who has ADHD.

Now that you know what it means to have ADHD, let's think about what it looks like for you.

What skill or talent comes easily to you? List three things that you're good at. Remember, James, Sammy, and Ella described their strengths earlier. For example, Sammy is super talented at drawing comics.

I'm good at:

1.

2.

3.

What things are harder for you? Think of them as "works in progress," meaning they can improve if you work on them.

Three things that are hard for me:

1.

2.

3.

Here are situations that can sometimes be harder for kids with ADHD.

Can you pick out which situations would be harder for James, Sammy, and Ella? Are any of them hard for you?

- I make careless mistakes on schoolwork (like rushing through instructions or forgetting to check my answers).
- If it's not fun, I have trouble paying attention.
- People have to call my name a few times before I hear them because I'm busy thinking about something else.
- It's hard for me to get started on something; when I do, I get sidetracked and don't finish.
- I have trouble keeping my stuff organized.
- I lose things that I need (like homework, pencils, or my jacket).
- It's hard for me to get my homework done.
- I get easily distracted by my daydreams or by what's going on around me.
- I have trouble sitting still.

- I have trouble remembering all the steps of daily routines (like getting ready in the morning or at bedtime).
- I leave my desk when I'm not supposed to.
- I climb or run when I'm not supposed to.
- I have a lot of energy, and I need to keep moving.
- I have trouble playing quietly.
- People say I talk a lot.
- I blurt out answers to questions.
- I have trouble waiting for my turn.
- I interrupt when other people are talking.

How can you work on these skills?

Different things work for different people. Here's what helps James, Sammy, and Ella.

Going to bed earlier, getting plenty of sleep, and eating a healthy breakfast in the morning gives me the energy to "get up and go."

It also helps when I lay out my school clothes, pack my backpack, and find my shoes and coat the night before.

My mom put up a to-do list that I check off as I get ready.

I need to get a lot of exercise, and my teacher gives me movement breaks during class to help get my wiggles out.

During recess, the teacher keeps an eye on me and reminds me to stay calm and to keep my hands to myself when I play.

Then I get a sticker on my chart. If my chart is full at the end of the week, I get to choose a prize!

It helped when my teacher moved my desk to the front of the room, away from the window. She checks to make sure I'm paying attention when she gives instructions, and she writes down what I'm supposed to do in case I miss a step.

I highlight the symbols in my math problems, so I don't add when I'm supposed to subtract, and I use a graphic organizer when I write.

I've also learned to speak up and ask for help and reminders when I need them!

Some kids with ADHD also take special medicine that helps them focus, sit still, and think before they act. This is something you can learn more about by talking to your parents and your doctor.

What three things would help you do better in situations that are hard for you?

1.

2.

3.

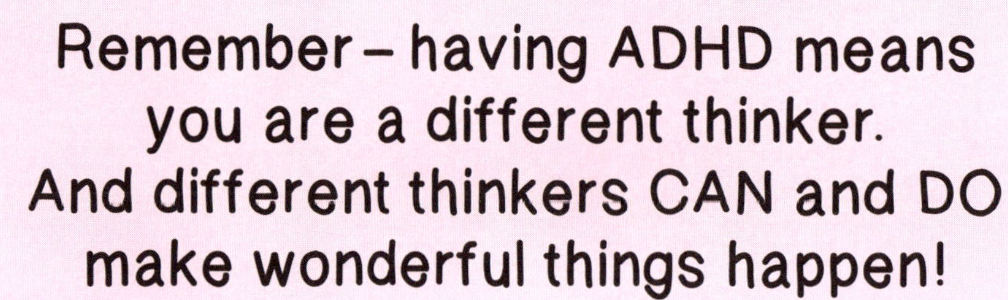
Remember – having ADHD means
you are a different thinker.
And different thinkers CAN and DO
make wonderful things happen!

TIPS for Parents, Caregivers, & Educators

Celebrating Different Thinkers

Encourage and empower children who have ADHD! Use these tips to help kids better understand their amazing brains so they can navigate the world around them even more successfully.

1 Make sure you are comfortable with this subject matter before reading the book with children. Kids are more likely to understand and identify with a diagnosis if their parents/caregivers/teachers are confident thinking and talking about it.

2 Use the prompts in the story ("Does this ever happen to you?") as opportunities to help kids explore and reflect on what it means to be a different thinker or have ADHD.

3 Think about how executive functioning skills work in day-to-day activities. Grocery shopping is a great example. The grocery store is a structured setting that can be navigated with ease. However, someone who struggles with planning and organization may find themselves wandering back and forth, forgetting things that they intended to purchase, and taking twice as long to complete their shopping. (For example, getting a cucumber, then grabbing some yogurt, then returning to the produce section for tomatoes.) Impulsivity also can interfere, which is why they put those chocolate bars in the checkout line! This is a relatable, real-life example you can share and discuss with kids.

4 Modify the discussion of neuroanatomy according to a child's developmental level. Some children may be interested in delving more deeply into this subject, while others may benefit from a more general, surface-level review.

5 Pause when the term ADHD is introduced and ask how familiar they are with the word. This is a good time to correct any misconceptions kids may have.

6 Encourage children to reflect on their own personal strengths, and share with them the strengths you see in them. Discuss how some of those strengths could be related to their different-thinking mind. For example, they may have an amazing imagination. We know that individuals with ADHD are often more creative.

7 Brainstorm together about next steps. Is there a plan when kids are at school? Will you meet with the pediatrician to discuss medication? Are routines in place at home and at school?

For more parenting information, visit:

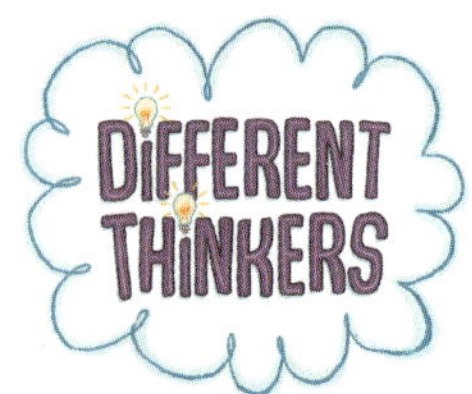

Boys Town Press Books to Build Lifelong Skills

Different Thinkers – Winner of Multiple Awards!

A series designed to guide and support neurodivergent children and their families as they work toward their life goals.

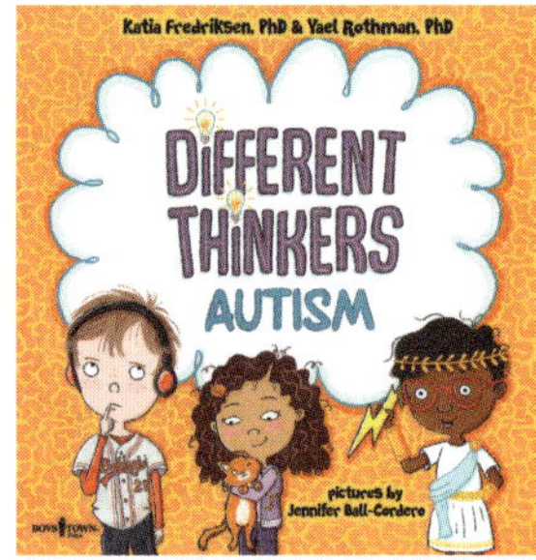

979-8-88907-024-5

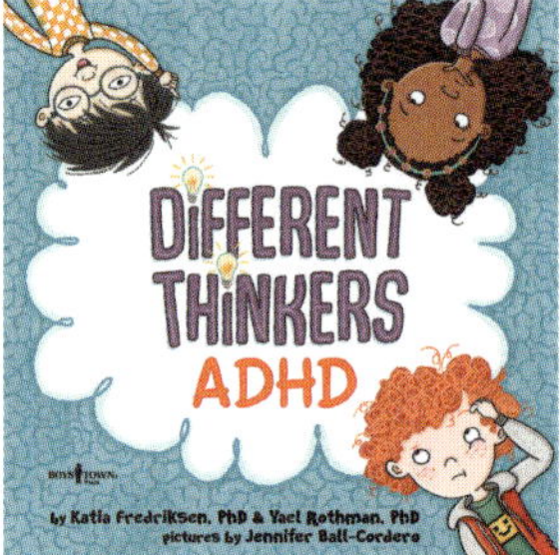

979-8-88907-006-1

More Praise for Different Thinkers: ADHD

"This easy read helps children better understand ADHD and associated problems with self-control. Complex concepts are explained using clear and simple language. The book does not gloss over the difficulties posed by ADHD but neither does it suggest that children should be defined by their disorders. Challenges and strengths are both discussed in realistic but positive terms. As a Developmental-Behavioral Pediatrician, I will enthusiastically recommend this very helpful book."

– DAN SHAPIRO, M.D.,
Developmental-Behavioral Pediatrician, creator of the Parent Child Journey and Excursions Programs

More to Explore!

978-1-944882-98-3

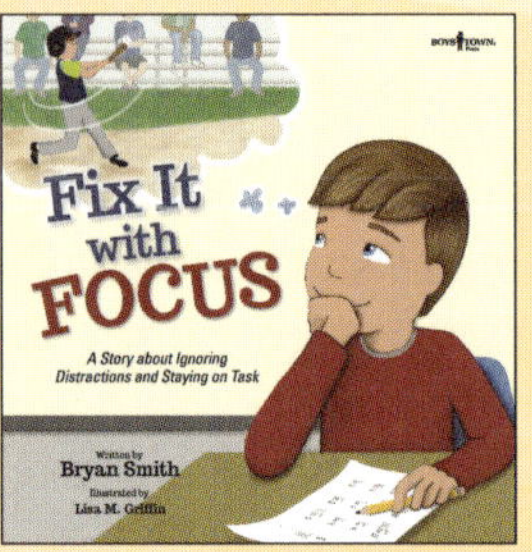

978-1-944882-60-0

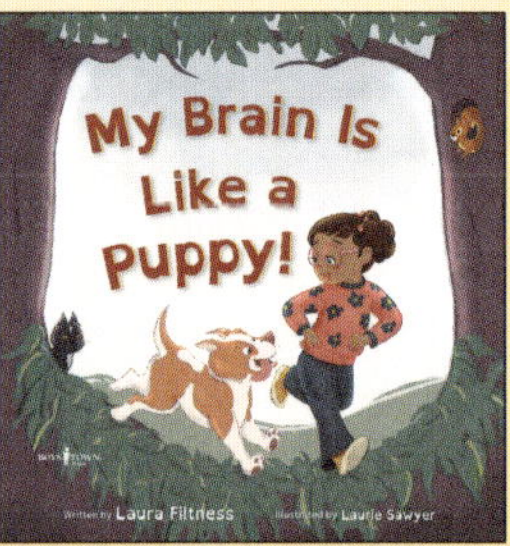

979-8-88907-036-8

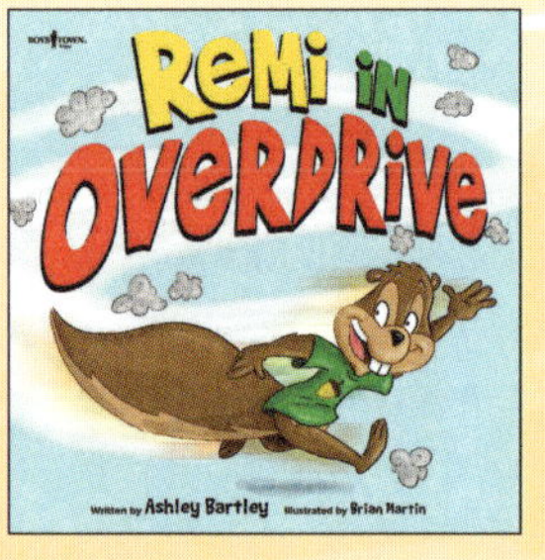

978-1-944882-87-7

For information on Boys Town and its Education Model, Common Sense Parenting®, and training programs:
LiftwithBoysTown.org | Parenting.org
training@boystown.org | 800-545-5771

For parenting and educational books and other resources:
BoysTownPress.org
btpress@boystown.org | 800-282-6657